THE
Archive Photographs
SERIES

ISLE OF SHEPPEY

'So modern, such luxury and elegance that it can only be the new steamship *Princess Juliana*.'
An advertisement for the Zeeland Steamship Company which operated a day and night service
between Queenborough and Vlissingen (Flushing) until 1914.

THE
Archive Photographs
SERIES

ISLE OF SHEPPEY

Compiled by
Nina Brigden Reid

Nina Brigden Reid
16.10.96

CHALFORD

First published 1996
Copyright © Nina Brigden Reid 1996

The Chalford Publishing Company
St Mary's Mill, Chalford,
Stroud, Gloucestershire, GL6 8NX

ISBN 0 7524 0394 X

Typesetting and origination by
The Chalford Publishing Company
Printed in Great Britain by
Redwood Books, Trowbridge

Contents

THE OLD AND NEW KINGSFERRY BRIDGES, ISLE OF SHEPPEY

On the right is the old bridge, built in 1904. The greatly improved new one, constructed by John Howard and Co Ltd, was opened by HRH the Duchess of Kent on 20 April 1960.

Nina Brigden Reid was born on the Isle of Sheppey. She comes from a naval family and had the first five years of her education in Sheerness. After a short spell as a civil servant in HM Dockyard she left to take a long close look at North America. Since then she has travelled widely in the UK and abroad.

A champion of her birthplace, she started to collect prints, postcards and ephemera quite casually, beginning with Sheerness but gradually ranging over the entire island. She has chosen 200 postcard images out of the thousand in her albums. It is a personal selection. Some are included for their historical interest or in contrast with the present, others out of nostalgia or for amusement only. Much of the pleasure in compiling the book has been in renewing old acquaintanceships and exploring parts of the island that she tended to neglect when she lived in Sheerness.

Many friends helped with family details, while discussions with Gwen Croally and Joyce Taylor supplied invaluable general information. The photograph on page 62 was kindly provided by Vera Evans. Thanks to the helpfulness of the staff, a day spent in the Sheerness Library archive was most productive. Telephone enquiries to Swale Borough Council were always dealt with sympathetically.

The Sheerness Heritage Centre is in a former dockyard matey's cottage at 10 Rose Street. It is now a Grade II listed building and a fitting reward for any visitor or resident who is anxious that some of the character of the old town should be preserved.

In June 1667, with the intention of burning 'King Charles's wig', a Dutch battle-fleet under Admiral de Ruyter sailed up the Medway and destroyed Upnor Castle. On the way they captured and occupied the island - *Het Eylandt Shepey* - and its fort at *Shirenasse*. An engraving published by Nicolas Fisher after W Schellinks's original drawings.

Introduction

Sheppey's isolated position in the Thames estuary at the mouth of the Medway gave it a special strategic importance from Roman times to the present century. Two years after Pepys reported that the local defences should be upgraded, de Ruyter sailed the Dutch fleet into the Medway in the summer of 1667, destroyed Sheerness fort and occupied the island for a few days. This was probably the most dramatic event in the island's history that includes many other stories ranging from the oft-repeated legend of the fourteenth-century Robert de Shurland and his horse to the factual and better-documented account of the 1797 naval Mutiny at the Nore.

Thousands of men and women remembered Sheppey as a place where they were stationed during their service in the navy, army or air force. Sheerness was predominantly a dockyard town while the armed forces were scattered over the island. Sheppey's economy suffered disastrously when the dockyard closed and the services departed.

The Isle of Sheppey is approximately ten by five miles of diverse terrain. A day spent on the

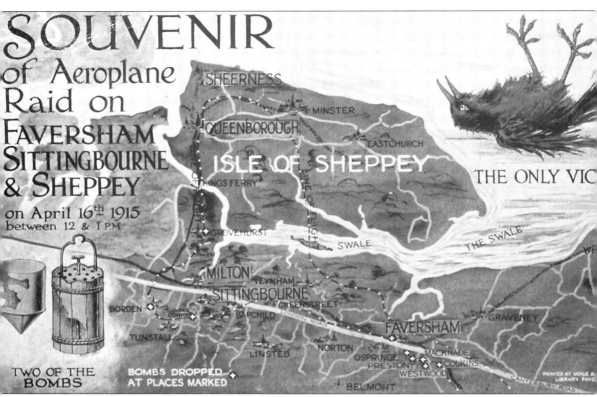

The Isle of Sheppey suffered casualties and damage from aerial bombardment in both great wars. With just one feathered casualty this aeroplane raid could be reported light-heartedly.

marshes in the south is a rewarding experience for any naturalist, but especially for the birdwatcher. To wander through Queenborough cannot help but awaken thoughts of Hogarth and Nelson on their respective travels. A visit to Blue Town and what remains of the dockyard revives images of their bustling heydays. There are still buildings, indeed whole streets in Sheerness that show how the town developed and its hundreds of dockyard workers lived.

Each year more of the cliffs at Minster and beyond are eroded but postcards record buildings and farmers' fields which, with Second World War gun emplacements and pillboxes, have tumbled into the sea, the victims of countless landslides.

The island is still popular with holiday-makers, especially those who enjoy the pleasures of both sea and countryside. Sheltered sailing in the River Swale brings new enthusiasts, while the usually persistent breeze attracts colourful flotillas of windsurfers to the island's north shore.

Sheppey's new, modern industries have a direct sea link with continental Europe by way of Vlissingen, and lively discussions are in progress about the advantages of a second road bridge connecting the island to the Kent mainland and the national motorway system. Further investment could return the island to something approaching its former prosperity.

Nina Brigden Reid
Kew Gardens

One
HM Dockyard and
Surrounding Area

Workmen handling a cargo c. 1905. Some dockyard buildings are visible to the right behind the high sea-wall.

Eagle and Queen Line Pleasure Steamers

"QUEEN OF THANET"

LEAVES

Margate Jetty

DAILY at 4.30 p.m.

(Fridays excepted)

Weather and other circumstances permitting

— FOR —

SOUTHEND
SHEERNESS

AND

CHATHAM

FARES :

		SINGLE	SEASON RETURN
To SOUTHEND	...	6/-	10/-
SHEERNESS	...	4/-	7/6
CHATHAM	...	5/-	8/6

Children under 14 years half-fare

Passengers are only carried on the terms and conditions printed on the Company's Tickets.

Free Admission to Jetty

Luggage accompanying passenger up to 100-lbs. free.

REFRESHMENTS ON BOARD   FULLY LICENSED

BOOK EARLY AT PIER HEAD

H. L. TOBY, PRINTER, MARGATE   No. 4

A handbill advertising the services of *The Queen of Thanet*, with the ominous small-print proviso 'Weather and other circumstances permitting.'

The first Sheerness pier opened in 1835. It was a working one where pleasure steamers called and a popular place to promenade. With so many naval vessels moored off-shore and the activity of commercial craft, there was always something of interest to see while taking refreshment at the end of the pier.

A hundred years later, Sheerness was still a busy port. When the tide was low local boys would stand alongside the pier calling 'Penny in the mud for a scramble'. By the end of the day they had collected quite a few hard-searched-for coins thrown to them by generous visitors.

During the winter of 1895 the rivers Medway and Swale froze, temporarily trapping a number of vessels in the ice.

Edward Holl designed the great Quadrangular Storehouse, identified by its clock-tower. It was just one of the nineteenth-century buildings demolished after HM Dockyard closed in 1960. The large building to the left housed the Gunnery School and later the shore training establishment HMS *Wildfire*.

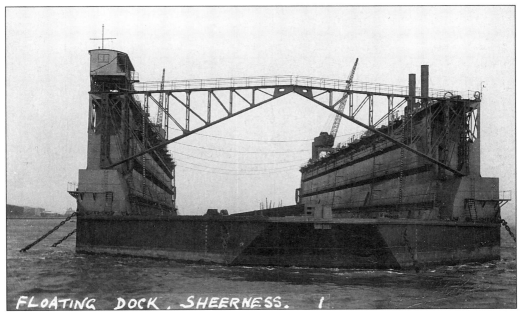

FLOATING DOCK, SHEERNESS. 1

A floating dock arrived at Sheerness early in the 1914-18 war. It was used to raise vessels out of the water to undergo repairs by dockyard workmen. On page 11 it can be seen at its mooring in the Medway.

Sea-Plane in Sheerness Harbour.

The sea-plane flying around Garrison Point and the harbour might well be one of the aircraft sponsored by the *Daily Mail* in 1912 to tour coastal resorts as part of Lord Northcliffe's efforts to promote an interest in aviation. At the extreme left are two Thames barges, for many years a familiar sight on the Medway.

Early in the 1890s, the Royal Navy founded a Gunnery School at Sheerness to train ratings from there and Chatham. Instruction was rigorous and included a detailed study of the manufacture and assembly of the guns as well as their use.

Blue-jackets laying out their kit in regulation order for inspection. The photograph was taken between October and April, for sailors wore white covers on their caps only from May until September until 1956. In Sheerness - as in other naval towns - it was recognised that summer had come when they came ashore wearing their white hats. Many children considered it a sign of good luck and made a wish when they saw their first of the season.

The official residence of the chief officer of the dockyard, the Captain Superintendent. An elegant house, built in the 1820s, it stands immediately inside the main entrance to the dockyard. Appropriately, a ship's figure-head of Admiral Nelson overlooked the entrance.

Above the Superintendent's Stairs stands the building that housed the offices of the Captain Superintendent, and in 1901 also those of the Chief Constuctor, Naval Storekeeper and Cashier. The steam pinnace by the steps is taking crews to and from ships moored in the harbour.

The twelve women proudly photographed must have been recruited to work in the Electrical Department to release men for service in the armed forces. Unfortunately no names are written on the reverse, only 'During Great War with Germany 1914-1918'.

No names again, but the group shows how closely naval and civilian lives interacted in the organisation of the dockyard and, inevitably, beyond its walls. The captain in the centre was probably the Captain Superintendent, perhaps the other naval officers were from ships in port at the time and the civilians were senior officers of the dockyard.

The inscription on this bronze commemorative medal surrounds a view of John Rennie's early plans. It tells us that the basin and docks at Sheerness were begun on 19 January 1814 and opened on 5 September 1823. The cost of the building and engineering work is said to have totalled £2,586,083 with an additional £50,000 for the high brick enclosing wall.

Workmen stream through the Main Gate. Dockyard police on duty were authorised to stop and search anyone leaving the yard.

Opposing football teams looking remarkably similar. The Civil Service Sports Club on the left, versus a team of Wrens (Women's Royal Naval Service) stationed at Sheerness. The friendly match was played on the sports ground of the old Range Accommodation buildings on Wednesday, 14 August 1948 and the score was 1-1. With the civil servants in dark blue and the Wrens in identical colours only the goalkeepers in white were readily distinguishable. The confused referee was Mr D Dorling.

The Duke of Clarence (later King William IV) greatly admired Rennie's plans for the port and the great dockyard buildings. He attended the official ceremony of The Opening of Sheerness Docks on 5 September 1823. Until his accession in 1830 the Duke considered taking up permanent residence in Admiralty House. In due course it became the official residence of the Commander-in-Chief at the Nore. Like so many nineteenth-century buildings in this area it was destroyed as the modern port developed.

The fort at Garrison Point commands the entrance to the River Medway. It was a predecessor of this nineteenth-century defence that surrendered to the Dutch admiral de Ruyter in 1667. Almost three centuries later, in 1940, hundreds of British and allied troops were brought into the harbour by small pleasure boats that rescued them from Dunkirk when France fell to the German army.

Dockyard Church, sometimes known as Garrison Church, has been allowed to fall into disrepair. Its architect, GL Taylor was also responsible for the Captain Superintendent's residence.

When church parade was compulsory in HM Forces it was impressive to hear hymns being heartily sung by a congregation composed mostly of soldiers and sailors. Before a church was established on this site in 1828, services were conducted on board a hulk tied up in the dock.

On the right-hand side of the old road from Blue Town to Sheerness was the entrance to Well Marsh where the army had its sports field, now the site of a steel works. The bollards at the roadside are the barrels of old cannon. Road development and the establishment of the Duke of Clarence Trading Estate have completely altered the area since this card was postmarked 1908.

Opposite Well Marsh, Garrison Road led to the Main Gate of the dockyard. It also passed the soldiers' barracks and parade ground, then Admiralty House before continuing to the fort. Four men of the Royal Garrison Artillery mount guard c. 1907. The tree-lined avenue behind them leads to Dockyard Church and the residential Naval Terrace.

The Sittingbourne-Sheerness railway opened in 1860 and operated via Kingsferry Bridge and Queenborough, terminating in Blue Town at Sheerness Dock Yard station near the South Gate.

A scene of devastation in 1909 after the White House Sailors' Home fire in Blue Town. A photographer was quick to capture this scene with some local children who had come to view the damage. Young as they are, they all wear hats.

"WHITE HOUSE" FIRE.

A description of the tragedy was given on 3 May 1909 by the sender of this card: "The photograph is the scene of our local fire recently, the place being known as the 'White House Sailors' Home'. As about 40 sailors were on the premises there were some thrilling and heroic escapes from the burning building in which one Royal Marine was found buried among the debris. The building contained one large room built many years ago as the first meeting place for Nonconformists in Sheerness."

An everyday street scene in West Minster c. 1906. The children were probably all playing in the street when the photographer arrived and gathered them together. The milkman has a churn on his horsedrawn cart and people would have milk ladled into their own jugs. As late as the 1940s tradesmen still delivered bread and vegetables by horsedrawn vehicles. The driver and his horse became friends to the community, and many people will still remember Mr Vic Wood of Humphrey's bakery and his horse "Queenie".

The Royal Fountain Hotel, built in 1812, accommodated many Admiralty officials visiting HM Dockyard, among them John Dickens, father of Charles, the Victorian novelist. As a pay clerk in Chatham Dockyard, Dickens *père* would have made frequent duty visits to Sheerness. During the Second World War The Fountain was a favourite place for off-duty naval officers to gather. Sadly, the building is no longer an hotel.

Built in 1873, St Paul's Church was the parish church of Blue Town. When it was demolished, in 1962, the congregation joined that of the Dockyard Church which then became known as St Paul's Dockyard Church.

The exterior of St Paul's belied its rather impressive interior.

Many ships' figureheads from men-of-war could be seen throughout the dockyard before its closure in 1960. A reproduction of one that adorned HMS *Forte* now stands at the base of the sea-defence wall in Marine Parade at the top of Richmond Street. The ship was last commissioned as the flagship of the East Indies, was paid off in 1872 and burnt at Sheerness in 1905.

Two
Sheerness Town

Perhaps the written message expresses what many servicemen thought during both wars when they found themselves on a previously unheard of British isle.

The moat was built as part of the defences of the dockyard and fort. The dockyard church tower looms in the distance and the guardroom stands at the far end of the bridge. Between 1903 and 1917 a tram service ran between the dockyard and Sheerness East with a branch line along the Broadway and on to Cheyney Rock.

Following the road past the Sheerness War Memorial an aerial view shows some military buildings once used to accommodate the garrison. These buildings have been destroyed and the space is now used by Medway Ports Limited for cargo storage.

UVEILING OF WAR MEMORIAL. SHEERNESS. 4

The Sheerness War Memorial, erected by voluntary subscription, was unveiled at 3 pm on Saturday, 29 April 1922, by Admiral Sir Hugh Evans-Thomas KCB KCMG MVO LLD, Commander-in-Chief at the Nore. The clergy in attendance were the Rev HCW Allinson, Vicar of Holy Trinity: the Rev EF Tozer, Alma Road Congregational Church: the Rev F Ellis, Salem Wesleyan: the Rev CJ Chamberlain, YMCA and Baptist Church; the Rev RJ Lubbock, Vicar of St Paul's and the Chaplain of HM Dockyard Church. After the ceremony the Chairman of the War Memorial Committee, Councillor WJ Thwaites JP, presented a copy of the Roll of Honour to the Urban District Council.

The dedication ceremony was well attended by the townspeople and after Councillor Thwaites laid a wreath from the Committee, they placed fresh flowers at the base of the memorial honouring 275 servicemen and civilians who died as a result of enemy action and the 77 dockyard employees working aboard the minelayer HMS *Princess Irene* on 27 May 1915, when an explosion ripped the vessel apart.

Another tragedy occurred early in the war when HMS *Bulwark* blew up in Sheerness harbour on 26 November 1914, with the reported loss of some 600 lives.

The London, Chatham and Dover Railway Company terminus at Sheerness-on-Sea, c. 1910. Unfortunately this wooden building was replaced by a standard British Rail design in 1971 after a train ploughed through the forecourt of the old station, killing one person and injuring seven others.

Not until 1883 was the rail service extended from Blue Town to the present Sheerness-on-Sea terminus. Steam locomotives were replaced by diesel electric in 1959.

Holiday-makers arriving by train could leave the station and immediately find the open sea at the far end of this walk. An amusement park is on the left. A Tesco store now stands on part of the ground where once dodgems and roll-a-penny stalls delighted visitors and residents alike.

Entering the High Street from the north-west where the Economical Society, established in 1816, advertises its dairy products and offers to cater for small parties. Curtiss and Sons of Blue Town transport goods to London and other naval and military towns. Stray dogs are ever present and the horse-and-cart is the commercial vehicle c. 1914.

The exterior of the Railway Hotel has changed little except its name since c. 1908. It is now The Fiddlers Cat, whose landlord could hardly muster such a dazzling array of uniforms for a photocall today. There is a marked absence of women in this scene save for, presumably, the barmaid in the front and two chambermaids on the balcony. The advertisement for Jude Hanbury and Company's Wateringbury Ales has been supplanted by a neon sign in a window for Budweiser.

Cork's Tobacco and Cigar Store, 16 and 18 High Street, c. 1907, also described itself as a Fancy Bazaar, which accounts for the half-dozen well-dressed young boys in the vicinity. The lad in the sailor suit appears to have made a purchase. In the 1930s Ancell's toy shop was equally attractive to the young when it occupied the same site on the corner of Beach Street.

Looking north-west along the High Street towards Blue Town, c. 1910. None of these shops exists now and the frontages have been completely changed. The pawnbroker's sign of three golden balls can be seen high on the left above 49 High Street. The shop belonged to Mr Sams in later years and on VE-night a high-spirited sailor managed to scale the building and dislodge the sign.

The first sight of a motor car, parked in the High Street outside the Woolworth store opened on 31 October 1925.

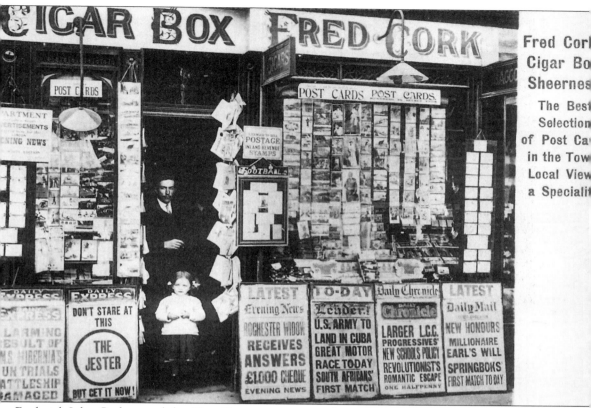

Frederick John Cork owned the Cigar Box, a stationers and newsagents at 51 High Street, and the Fancy Repository at 16 and 18 High Street. He produced dozens of Cork's Invicta Series of local view postcards which were sent all over the world. The placards in this one, posted to California in 1910, establish that the photograph was taken during the first weeks of 1906.

Carcasses hang outside Penney the family butchers in 1906 when it was not uncommon for pigs still to have their heads on when displayed. The business at 73 High Street was founded by Mr Penney in the second half of the nineteenth century. His son Frederick took over in 1911 and the shop closed during the second world war. The Britannia Hotel is to the left and the Bon Marche Drapery Company to the right, both buildings now house different businesses.

In 1912 the Bon Marche drapery store made deliveries by wooden handcart. A number of the buildings around the clock, in the area known as The Crescent were still private dwellings in the early 1900s.

The Coronation Memorial Clock, built in 1902 to commemorate the enthronement of King Edward VII and Queen Alexandra stands at the spiritual centre of the town. Its decorative gas-lamps have long since disappeared. Proposals to remove the town clock to ease the traffic flow met with successful opposition from residents and ex-pats alike. This card was No. 1 in the "Excelsior" series produced by Cole, a local printer and stationer.

The High Street, Sheerness-on Sea.

Daily activity in the town centre c. 1910. A policeman controls the traffic; passengers wait at the No. 6 stop for a tram advertising Featherstone's, the furnishers in the Broadway. The Maypole Dairy receives a delivery from the Machine Bakery, fodder for the horse hanging at the back of the van.

Sir Edward Banks, one of Rennie's contractors for rebuilding the dockyard in the early 1800s, was responsible for the development of this area of the town. So strong was his influence that it was known locally as Banks Town. The ground floors of the houses in the Broadway, first known as Edward Street, are now shops and offices.

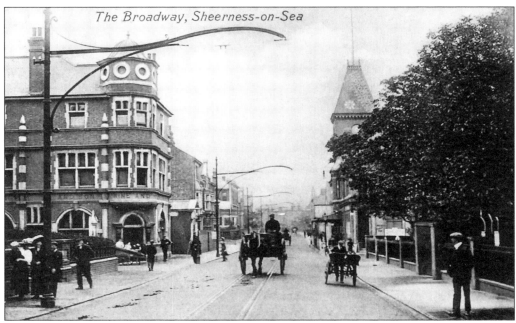

The Broadway, Sheerness-on-Sea

The Royal Hotel, c. 1910, another of Sir Edward's designs, was built in 1827 as a private residence called Kent House. It stands on the corner of Royal Road. Nearby Delamark Road was named after Banks's son.

A popular social centre, especially during the days of full employment in HM Dockyard, the Working Men's Club and Institute has occupied this building since 1882.

The Hippodrome c. 1907 with its glass-covered arcade and tower that dominates the Broadway skyline. This home of entertainment has been replaced by the Midland Bank and offices that include those of The Sheerness Times Guardian.

The Argosy and Rio cinemas opened in two consecutive years, 1936 and 1937. In the days before television, when films were the most popular form of entertainment, queues for admission were a common sight. Both buildings were occasionally used for public gatherings, notably the Argosy for a meeting of shareholders when the Hastings and Thanet Building Society made a successful takeover bid for the Sheerness and Gillingham Permanent Building Society. The Argosy is now a bingo hall and a block of flats has replaced the Rio.

The Conservative Club in The Broadway, c. 1911. The tram dominates the road while there is abundant evidence of horse traffic. Built in 1897, the club remains unchanged.

Holy Trinity Church was part of the Banks Town scheme: built in 1835-36 the architect was GL Taylor. It has always been popular for Church of England weddings. The cast-iron railings taken for recycling during the Second World War were replaced recently.

In Trinity Road, the town's only formal park provides a peaceful retreat on a sunny day in 1934.

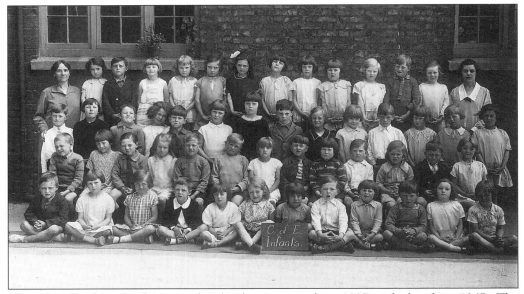

The Church of England National School was opened in 1837 and closed in 1967. The classrooms and playground were behind Holy Trinity church and school life had close links with it. These children, photographed in 1929 are probably two infant classes, girls outnumbering boys that year. Miss Reeves, the headmistress stands on the left.

Lunchtime in 1930 when schoolchildren could walk home in safety for their midday meal.

Miss Reeves on the right and Miss Dover, the class teacher. Pupils of this 1931 class will remember not only how strict the discipline was but also how thorough the teaching practices were of the dedicated staff.

In the summer term school plays were performed in the playground. These aspiring thespians are members of the Junior School in 1937.

Here, Mr John West and his wife, Elizabeth, are at the front of the antique and second-hand furniture shop they established at 138 High Street in 1908. They had interests all over the island, and a cousin, Mrs Harris kept donkeys for children to ride on the sands.

The West family, mother, father and six children, have been summoned to stand outside the double-fronted premises in 1921, before the later renovations took place. Little Grace holds her mother's hand.

A page from the June 1886 issue of the Sheppey Church Monthly Magazine: one penny a copy or 1/6d per annum post free. Ride's Great Mill almost opposite West and Sons was demolished in 1924 but the octagonal base can still be seen from the High Street.

The Alma Road Congregational Church built in 1859 was destroyed by fire in 1942. At the time it had a flourishing youth club, enjoyed by many denominations, which was greatly missed. Private houses now stand on the site.

A number of straight, uniform streets like Alma Road were built in the early 1900s. Leading to the sea-front they were popular in the 1930s with visitors wanting bed and breakfast.

St Helen's Road during the flood of February 1953. The island was cut off and supplies were brought in by boat and helicopters landing on the garrison parade-ground. Residents appreciated the advantage of living in a service town in an emergency when boats and military lorries delivered food and water to marooned households. Once the water subsided, clearing-up was a depressing task. Despite the disaster, no plans to reinforce the island's sea-defences were forthcoming until after the storms of 1978-79, when a decision was made to build the high sea-wall that now protects Sheerness but has so completely destroyed the quaint aspect of the old sea front.

All seaside towns should have good fresh fish shops. Sheerness had several, including Uncle Tom's Cabin in the High Street between St George's Avenue and Victoria Street. W. Worsley and his son, the proprietors, also fried fish and chips. Mr Rogers, another local fishmonger, went round the streets daily in the 1920s and 30s, his pushcart laden with a fresh catch and, in the summer, a mound of pink and brown shrimps.

The offices of the Sheerness Urban District Council in Trinity Road, c. 1905. The tall waterworks building on the left bears the wording Sheerness Local Board of Health. Beyond it the present Sheerness District Office of the Swale Borough Council is housed.

Medal in white metal presented to schoolchildren by the council as a souvenir of the coronation of King George V and Queen Mary, 22 June 1911. The heraldic devices on the reverse represent Kent and the Sheerness naval connection, the sea and the defence of England.

A bird's eye view of the Broadway looking east, c. 1924. Behind the look-out tower is the Boys' Technical School which was opened in 1910, closed in 1970 and demolished in 1975. The most famous of the future engineers and scientists who had their schooling there was Lord Penney OM KBE FRS, the atomic scientist, who was a pupil in the 1920's when Dr Bell was headmaster.

Boys of the Junior Technical School in their bold black and white ties.

Three
Sport and Entertainment

AT SHEERNESS

WE'RE SPLASHING IT

Day trips to the seaside were popular in the 1920s and 30s. As Sheerness was within easy reach of south London the delights of a dip in the briny were presented as irresistible.

BANDSTAND AND PAVILION, SHEERNESS

This was the last pavilion and bandstand complex to be built. Opened in the summer of 1924, for many years it housed visiting concert parties, local amateur shows, repertory companies and military bands. The people around the railing watch a game of bowls c. 1930, but perhaps those sitting in the shelter had the greatest pleasure as they critically observe the evening strollers on the promenade. The sea-defence wall obscures this view now. The pavilion and bandstand have been replaced by landscaped gardens.

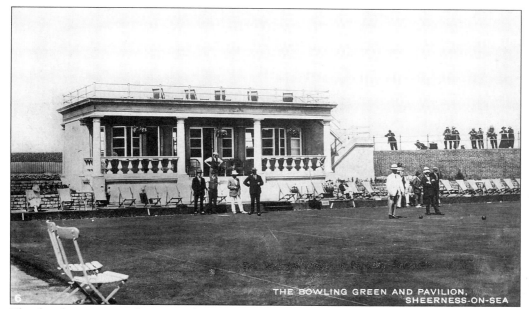

The bowling green, also opened in 1924, was enjoyed by spectators as well as players. A telescope on the club-house roof gave a splendid view across the estuary to Southend-on-Sea. A car park has replaced the green while the Coastal Studies Centre occupies the club-house.

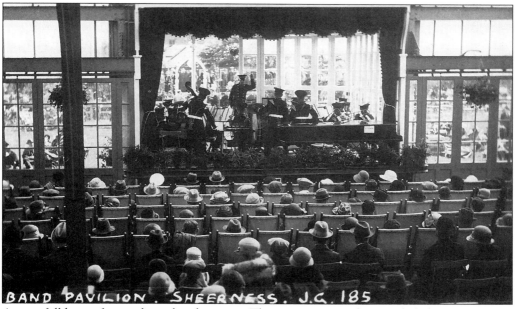

A near-full house for a military band concert. The programme perhaps included "A Life on the Ocean Wave" one of the popular compositions by a son of Sheppey, Henry Russell (1813-1900).

The Boating Lake c. 1930 was also affectionately known as the Paddling Pond. Wooden paddle-boats were powered by hand and if rescue was called for a white-coated attendant would wade in and pull boat and occupants to safety.

Annual visits by the same concert parties ensured that many entertainers became familiar friends of the town. When The Bouquets appeared at the Sheerness Pavilion in August 1939, the Carnival Queen was crowned on the stage of the Hippodrome by Miss Pearl Joyce, the company's contralto.

EMPIRE ENTERTAINERS.

The Empire Entertainers were typical of small companies who gave much pleasure during the summer months in dozens of Britain's seaside towns and were an important feature of the holiday-makers' calendar. The cast, who were expected to act, sing, dance, and recite monologues, were even more sought after if they could play an instrument. Backstage conditions were often far from ideal and finding seasonal lodgings in town was hazardous, but in this regard many lifetime friendships were established.

Sea View Gardens, Sheerness-on-Sea.

A white-coated deck-chair attendant collects his money in Sea View Gardens while a military band plays on, c. 1920.

TENNIS COURTS, MARINE GARDENS SHEERNESS. J.G. 193

Many summer sports were catered for. The ever popular tennis courts close to the sea front in Marine Gardens are now part of the sports centre complex.

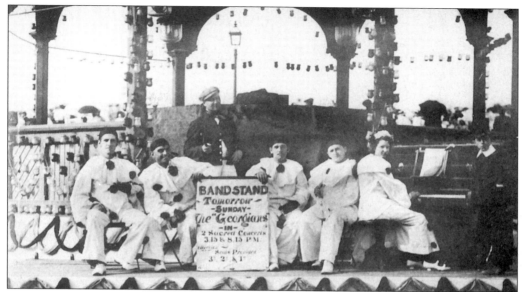

As their 1906 billboard announces, Sunday performances by The Original Georgians were devoted to sacred music, seats cost threepence, twopence and one penny.

In 1908 bandstand concerts were free for as many people as paid to hear them.

Between the wars Regatta Day brought crowds to the beach by the Catholic church. Local crews tested their strength, stamina and skills in a variety of sports against each other and the Royal Navy. Onlookers loved the Sweep and Miller: rowing boats with two men standing in each bombarded their opponents with paper bags full of soot or flour until one boat inevitably capsized. Environmentally unfriendly, perhaps, but great fun to watch.

Steam-pinnaces carrying the regatta judges are anchored in the bay. A message on the card records that one of them is *The Pride of Sheppey*.

The Hippodrome Buildings, completed in 1851. Another venue for visiting entertainers and local leisure activities, it was also used as a cinema in the 1930s. The elegant lamp standard disappeared long ago, the buildings more recently.

A motor-boat trip was the highlight of a day at the seaside.

On the 1000 yards firing line Sheerness Rifle Range

The Rifle Range was a small naval establishment on the edge of the fields behind Barton's Point. It was reached by a dirt track from the Halfway Road or by a rope-drawn ferry across the canal where there is now a wooden footbridge. A busy training area, it was also used for British service rifle meetings, by visiting forces from overseas and civilian rifle clubs.

Muster at Sheerness Rifle Range

A contingent from the United States Navy and Marines shot there in 1920.

An ambitious production of *The Pirates of Penzance*. Many photographs of Sheppey theatrical groups like this were taken by Lilian Mason, who had a studio in Minster.

The Sheerness Co-operative Choral Society, 1926. Composed of members of staff and customers, their concerts and operetta productions delighted audiences for years. Mr Harold Amor in the centre of the front row was the group's conductor and inspiration, on his right sits the pianist Mrs Ada Woodthorpe. Mr Albert Brightman, fourth man from the left, was Sheerness Pier- and Harbourmaster, and choirmaster at the Dockyard Church.

An exciting day for Sheerness, the official opening of the Aquarena on 24 August 1939. After many months when the council debated surveyors' reports, applications for tenders and costs, it must have been a relief to all when at last the project was completed. Lord Harris of Belmont declared the Aquarena open and is seen on the left helping Miss Bunty Bownes, a champion of the local swimming club, into the pool. As the ladies' hats testify, it was a social occasion of some importance for the island's worthies. A comment on a predecessor of the Aquarena appeared in the *United Service Journal* of 20 December 1833: "A handsome edifice has just been erected within a few yards of the beach to contain hot and cold baths and every convenience required."

Four
The Sea-front

A young girl rides along the esplanade in a goat-cart, c. 1910. The ornate shelter was a haven for strollers when the wind was in the north-east.

The Esplanade & Sands, Sheerness-on-Sea.

Cork's Invicta Series. Photo by Fred Cork.

When Mr Cork produced this card c. 1908, few people had their own cameras. The professional couple with an array of bulky photographic equipment took rather formal pictures of individuals or groups who would then have a record of their visit to Sheerness.

THE ESPLANADE, SHEERNESS

Looking west along the esplanade c. 1935 the big wheel in the Amusement Park stands boldly against the sky. A string of coloured lights provide summer evening illumination. Beach photographers were always busy in this area. On the left their subjects queue to collect their pictures.

64

This image is typical of its period, 1931. A local mother and little girl share the pleasures of a summer's day walk. Dressed in white, both wear hats and the mother stockings too; a sharp contrast to the clothes of a similar pair taking a seaside stroll today. Photography by itinerant cameramen continued until the outbreak of the war in 1939 when Sheerness became a restricted area where all photography in public places was controlled.

The Esplanade, Sheerness-on-Sea.

Looking over the water towards Southend from a crowded esplanade in the 1930s. A tearoom on the left, in the foreground concrete pillboxes, relics of the First World War.

Marine Parade Sands. Sheerness-on-Sea.

Girls paddle while boys sail their toy yachts c. 1912. On the horizon a paddle steamer makes its way to Margate. Nearer the beach two youngsters operate unusual 'water-bicycles'. Even on a summer's day the children in the sea shed few of their clothes.

The base of the '100 Acre Windmill' still stands in the grounds of the Seaview Hotel. It last ground the island's corn in 1872 and was dismantled six years later.

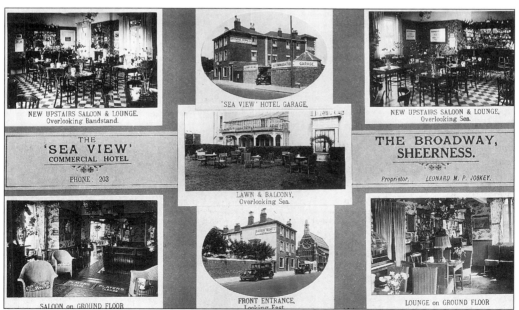

NEW UPSTAIRS SALOON & LOUNGE.
Overlooking Bandstand.

'SEA VIEW' HOTEL GARAGE.

NEW UPSTAIRS SALOON & LOUNGE.
Overlooking Sea.

THE
'SEA VIEW'
COMMERCIAL HOTEL

PHONE: 203

THE BROADWAY,
SHEERNESS.

Proprietor,   LEONARD M. P. JOSKEY.

LAWN & BALCONY.
Overlooking Sea.

SALOON on GROUND FLOOR

FRONT ENTRANCE.
Looking East.

LOUNGE on GROUND FLOOR

During the 1930s and 40s Mr and Mrs Joskey of the Sea View Commercial Hotel welcomed many visitors to their bar, year after year, frequently greeting them by name and remembering where they came from.

This was a familiar sight when walking past the Catholic church in a north-east gale. Dodging the spray was a good, if dangerous game to play. The look-out structure known as the Pepper Pot left a sad gap when it was taken down in the 1930s.

The Roman Catholic Church of SS Henry and Elizabeth can be seen clearly from the shipping channel in the mouth of the Thames, a welcome sight for sailors returning to England after a foreign service commission of two or three years.

The impressive interior of the Roman Catholic church. Built in 1863 it is considered a fine example of the work of Edward Welby Pugin (1834-75). Though somewhat weather-beaten it looks much the same today as it did c. 1906.

New Jetty, Sheerness. 98569

The stone jetty, c. 1925, was a favourite place for boys to fish with a hand line using mussels for bait. They rarely caught more than inedible crabs. On the frequent occasions when a young angler fell in Mr Davidson, known to all as Donald, invariably seemed to be on hand to rescue him.

Marine Parade, Sheerness-on-Sea.

Only a low wall protects Marine Parade from the sea c. 1910. In the distance a vessel unloads its cargo alongside the Co-operative coal pier. Opened in 1878, it was partly destroyed intentionally in 1939-40 for fear that invading Germans might make use of it. It has now been removed.

A card by Whalebone, 'Postcard King', Sheerness, c. 1910. Such a large gathering of children of different ages dressed in their best clothes suggests a Sunday school outing. This was the highlight of many a child's year and the day would certainly end with a tea-party in a church hall. The substantial houses of Marine Parade and pink-bricked Shrimp Terrace remain virtually unchanged since they were built.

A busy beach scene a few weeks before the outbreak of the First World War. As sea bathing became increasingly fashionable the more adventurous visitor could hire a bathing-tent and change into a modest costume before venturing into the waves.

Shrimp Terrace exposed to the elements in this Valentine Series from around 1904. The boys with the home-made wheelbarrow have probably been collecting driftwood.

A rising tide drives holiday-makers off the shore onto the beach steps, c. 1935. A promenade wall and concrete breakwaters protect Marine Parade. Windows of the Victoria Hotel on the right show why it was known locally as the Glasshouse. Now called Richmond House, it is occupied by a property management specialist.

The Grotto was built of barrels of Portland cement solidified by sea water when the ship carrying them ran aground in the latter half of the last century. Flint and Company operated licensed premises in the nearby wooden building where previously there had been a Coastguard station.

Flint's Ship on Shore, next to the Grotto, was a public house much frequented by off-duty sailors from Barton's Point rifle range. An added attraction c. 1936 was the stall offering locally-gathered cockles, winkles, mussels and jellied eels to accompany a glass of Fremlin's ale.

A walk along the shore from Sheerness to the White House Cafe was re-routed when there was firing at the rifle range. A look-out directed people along a covered way until the red flag was lowered.

Five
Parades and Celebrations

Thames Pageant fleet illuminated off Sheerness Thursday July 22, 1909. Naval pageantry was an important part of island life.

Celebrations marking the centenary of the Economical Society were delayed by the war until 1919. Founded in 1816 by volunteer officers and men of HM Dockyard, the society bought in bulk supplies of wheaten bread, flour and butcher's meat, and sold them to members at cost. Later water, an expensive commodity, was added to the list. The society expanded and flourished, so that by 1838 it was forced to replace the volunteer labour with paid employees. The rules remained strict and the principle of making just enough profit to cover expenses continued to be observed. In 1849 a rival co-operative was founded and the first joint meeting of the Sheerness Co-operative Society was held in 1875.

A solemn wild west entry for the Sheerness Carnival: a card dated 13 August 1924 by J Griffith of Alma Road. The portly man with the donkey and balloons appears to have better captured the spirit of the occasion.

Representatives of seasonal sports, tennis, cricket, golf, hockey, association football and bowls take their place in the carnival parade beneath Mr Sams' pawnshop sign.

Following the drum. The women's section of the Sheerness Labour Party parades past the Goat Hotel, Freeman Hardy and Willis, and Hounsell Brothers, the builders' merchants and ironmongers trading from 22-24 High Street.

The *Daily Herald* newspaper published its first edition on 25 January 1911, its last on 14 September 1964. A strong supporter of socialist ideals it sponsored Labour Party rallies throughout the country. In an attempt to boost sales by appealing to the whole family it introduced children's characters like Bobby Bear, Ruby Rabbit and Maisie Mouse who pose here above a dignified group from the Women's Section of the Sheerness Labour Party.

The months following the end of the First World War saw many celebratory events. Was the "Roasting of an Ox" on 26 July 1919 at Sheerness East part of one?

Boy Scouts celebrate the Coronation of King George V and Queen Mary, Sheerness, 22 June 1911. A year later Aunt Ethel used this card to tell Eric Cumberlege about the Scouts' relay race in the "jolly good" Artillery Sports.

Ye Olde True Brit...

Victory Street, S...

Sheppey has always had her fair share of public houses. In their heyday, those in Sheerness in particular drew much of their custom from the services. Elsewhere on the island pubs were havens where holiday-makers could relax after a day on the beach or in the country-side. Naturally, the residents cherished their own locals such as The True Briton which has served generations of patrons on the same site in Victory Street, Sheerness.

Six
Queenborough

The castle as it might have looked in the 1360s when it was visited by Edward III. After the king made the town a free borough in honour of Phillipa, his consort, its name was changed from Bynnee to Queenborough.

During the interregnum of 1649-60, the castle was considered outdated as a defence for the island. It was dismantled and the materials sold for re-use, some going to pave Whitehall. Water from the castle well was renowned for its purity and at one time was supplied to naval vessels calling at Sheerness. Queenborough railway station was built on the site of the castle and its grounds.

The Sheppey Light Railway was officially opened on 1 August 1901 and closed on 2 December 1950. For almost half a century it served the rural areas the length of the island from Queenborough to Leysdown.

Don't be Alarmed,

the

KING'S ROYAL RIFLES

are

" On Guard "

at

QUEENBOROUGH

The first World War brought many regiments to Sheppey for training and coastal guard duties before leaving this country for France. On 1 March 1916 a soldier of The King's Royal Rifle Corps posted this card to his "Darling Mother" in London, hoping to see her at the weekend and sending kisses to Horace his baby brother.

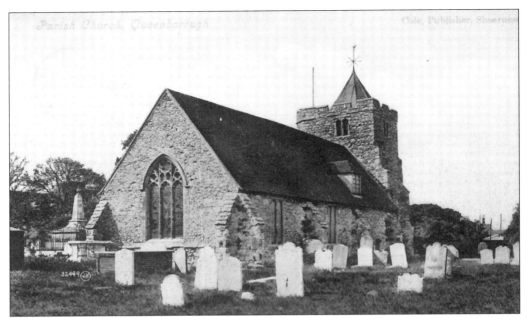

Admiral Nelson worshipped in Holy Trinity, the parish church of Queenborough, when his ship was in the lower Medway. He slept in Church House on the night before he sailed for Trafalgar. The church building dates in part from 1366. Its octagonal font of 1610 shows a contemporary representation of the castle gate.

Looking south-east from the church tower c. 1912. The factory buildings in the distance - glueworks, potteries and glassworks - have given employment to generations of families.

The 1793 Guildhall still stands in the High Street, a reminder of the historical importance of this little town. The man on the ladder checks the mantle and cleans the glass shade of the single gas-lamp that lit this long section of the street in 1906.

Looking along the High Street from the West Swale the Guildhall with its prominent clock stands on the left. The white building beyond the winter trees was destroyed during a Second World War air raid. Many people know this view from the sketch by William Hogarth (1697-1764), drawn when he "perambulated" the Isle of Sheppey with his friends in 1732.

The Sheerness Royal Dockyard Brigade was raised c. 1848 to help defend the Thames estuary. It was a locally-recruited unit of almost 900 men, much like today's Territorial Army. In 1852 Lt-Colonel Read led the brigade in a mock amphibious raid on neighbouring Queenborough watched by professional soldiers and by civilians with little idea of what was happening. Captain Flynn's boats, "fitted for the service of embarking and disembarking troops", carried

Major Laws' gunners and the infantry commanded by Major Freeman. The band of HMS
Monarch played them off as they sailed from their dockyard base "in excellent order", and
welcomed them back to the tune of "Rule Britannia". They formed up in companies in the yard
before marching out into Blue Town.

Shipping in the West Swale, c. 1911, where sail and steam still work side-by-side. The Queenborough oyster beds provided a significant source of income for the borough during the eighteenth century and the early years of the nineteenth. Their failure through mismanagement led to a marked decline in the prosperity of the inhabitants.

In the creek sailing barges could unload their cargoes directly onto the wharf. This area was recently developed at a cost of £226,000. The card is 3840 in the Milton "Glazette" series, a free gift with a loaf of bread in 1909.

In 1875 a railway branch line was opened between the town and the pier in the hope of attracting more passengers to the Zeeland line's passenger and mail service between Queenborough and Flushing. A Hall Series card.

A pier was in use at Queenborough before one was opened at Blue Town in 1835. *The Times* of 12 March 1894 reports a day of rejoicing in the borough when Princess Louise of Prussia arrived at Queenborough pier in the Royal Yacht. She was on her way to London to be married later that week to the Duke of Connaught, Queen Victoria's favourite son. During the Second World War the pier was a minesweeper base but fell into disrepair and was demolished in 1955.

This dramatic image by W Goodall, a local photographer, records the demolition of a works chimney. In the background are Queenborough Castle mound and the railway station. The card, bearing birthday greetings from Bert and Bertha, is postmarked 23 March 1915.

Seven

Minster

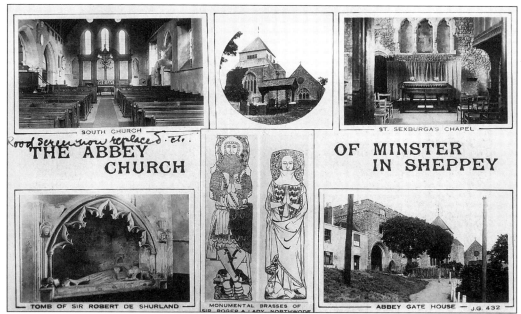

THE ABBEY CHURCH — SOUTH CHURCH · ST. SEXBURGA'S CHAPEL — OF MINSTER IN SHEPPEY — TOMB OF SIR ROBERT DE SHURLAND · MONUMENTAL BRASSES OF SIR ROGER & LADY NORTHWODE · ABBEY GATE HOUSE — J.G. 432

Rood Screen now replaced. etc.

The Abbey Church dates from c. 675, when Queen Sexburga founded a religious house for seventy-seven nuns of the order of St Benedict and became its first abbess. The convent was destroyed by the Danes, but was rebuilt c. 1130.

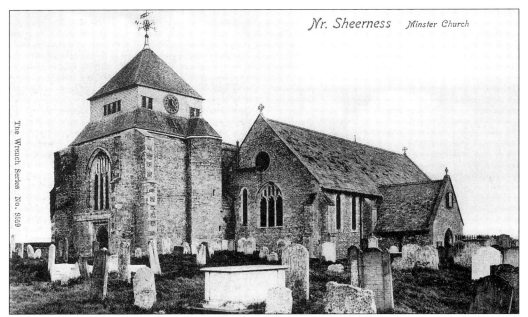

Nr. Sheerness *Minster Church*

Monuments in the Abbey Church, the parish church of Minster, commemorate the island's aristocracy while, outside, the headstones of lesser beings tell their stories. To make grass-cutting easier they have been placed around the perimeter of the churchyard where they are rapidly disappearing under an invasion of elder and ivy.

The Abbey Gate House is all that remains of the monastic foundation. It now houses the local history museum. In the 1930s the headstones still identified individual burial plots.

92

Pallida Mors æquo pulsat pede
Pauperum Tabernas Regumque Turres.

Whoe'er thou art, if here by Wifdom led
To view the filent manfions of the Dead;
To fearch for truth from life's laft mournful page,
Where Malice ftings not, nor where Slanders rage;
Read on:–No Bombaft fwells thefe friendly lines
Here truth unhonored and unvarnifhed fhines,
Where o'er yon Sod an envious nettle creeps,
From care efcaped–an honeft Gunner fleeps,
As on he travelled to life's forrowing end,
Diftrefs for ever claim'd him as a friend;
Orphan and Widow were alike his care,
He gave with pleafure all he had to fpare,
Deep in the Earth his Carcafe lies entomb'd,
Which Love and Grog for him had honeycomb'd,
His match now burnt, expended all his priming,
He left the World and us without ere whining,
Jefting apart, Retired from wind and Weather,
Virtue and WORTH are laid afleep together.

This Stone was Erected by
(as a Tribute of Friendship)
to the Memory of Mr HENRY WORTH,
GUNNER; who died Augt the 26th
1779, Aged 57 Years.
RENOVATED BY THE OFFICERS OF
SHEERNESS GARRISON. NOVr 1880.

OLD TOMBSTONE,
MINSTER, SHEPPEY. J.G. 461

It would be sad if the noble sentiments expressed on Henry Worth's headstone, decorated as it is with the tools of a gunner's trade and rich in artillery-men's puns are lost to future visitors, for it is no longer to be seen in the churchyard. It was signed by the stonemason Millen and Company, Sheerness.

As neither Sheppey nor her towns and villages have an officially recognised coat of arms the makers of seaside souvenirs turned to the heraldic devices of one of the island's more distinguished sons. Postcards and dozens of different patterns of Goss, Willow, Carlton and other crested chinawares are decorated with a version of the arms, crest and supporters of Sir Thomas Cheyne KG of Shurland, who has an imposing alabaster monument in the Abbey Church.

This general view of Minster village c. 1914 can still be captured from the island's lower road. New private houses and bungalows now cascade down the slope and many of the older buildings have disappeared.

Minster Hill in the early 1930s: the motor car is beginning to make a frequent appearance but roadside parking is not yet a problem and it is still relatively safe to push prams on the highway.

CE Butterfield, grocer and draper, was well situated on a corner where the High Street ends and Minster Road begins.

Two ladies take a winter stroll up Minster Road towards the Abbey Church. On their left they pass Prospect Villa, where Charles Dickens visited and which still stands among the many new houses. The "School - Caution" sign is topped by Invicta, the rampant-horse emblem of Kent. The card is postmarked 1911.

Since this card was printed c. 1925, the pond at Ward's Farm has been drained and filled and the site developed.

Carters drive in the middle of Station Road, confident that their right-of-way will not be challenged.

Brecknock Hill: or is it "breakneck"? The cartographers are uncertain.

Around 1926 the Glen was a pleasant place for a walk and a quiet picnic. It still is, although the surroundings are now more park-like than this picture shows.

This band cheered on what the writer of the card called the "drooping figures" of The Queen's Westminster Rifles during exercises at Minster in 1910.

AJ Dale, an East Minster photographer, thought the officers' mess and its sentry-box worth recording.

THE CLIFFS, MINSTER.

As late as 1950 there were few buildings on the cliffs and no road fit for motor cars. In the spring there were wildflowers in abundance and everywhere the song of skylarks.

Minster Cliffs

Erosion of the island's cliffs has always been a problem. A serious landslip that took an acre into the sea was reported in *The Illustrated London News* in 1870. The beach below the cliffs is a rewarding spot for fossil-hunters.

Minster village from the west c. 1903.

Norwood Farm (Manor) high on the island near Kingsbury Hill between Minster and Eastchurch c. 1907. In 1894 it was the home of Alfred Coultrip, a tireless campaigner for the rights of farm labourers, especially those affecting the welfare of men too old to work. Successive occupants have made alterations to the building: windows have been changed and the porch is now surmounted by a pitched roof. The people relaxing in the garden have a superb view across open fields and marshland to the River Swale and beyond.

The oaks that formed an avenue from the Royal Oak Hotel to the cliff edge have toppled into the sea. It was a rash motorist who ventured beyond this point.

Before the Royal Oak joined the oak trees at the foot of the cliffs, a walk from Sheerness ending in a clamber up the steep slope from the beach, might be rewarded with a drink in its tiny bar where one of the seats was an invalid's commode. Originally an isolated farmhouse it was reputed to have strong links with smugglers.

The techniques used to sell Minster building plots to city dwellers in the early part of this century can be compared to the "time-share" campaign operated in its closing years. Mr Ramuz, a local businessman was behind the scheme and it would appear that he was highly successful.

POST CARD.

Halfpenny

Stamp.

MINSTER-ON-SEA.

The New Health Resort. The most picturesque part of the beautiful Isle of Sheppey. Miles of quiet and interesting cliff walks. Free from restrictions. Splendid opportunities for bathing. Magnificent and extensive views. Frequent Excursions, : **3/6** return, including Luncheon. :

Full Particulars and Booklet Free.

DEVELOPMENT CORPORATION,
———— 68, Cheapside, E.C. ————

Eight
Eastchurch

All Saints Church c. 1906. Among the interesting tombs in the fifteenth-century parish church is that of Vice-Admiral Sir Richard King Bt KCB, Commander-in-Chief at the Nore, who died in Admiralty House, Sheerness, during the 1834 cholera epidemic.

The memorial erected in 1955 in recognition of the first home of British aviation stands in the village centre by the road leading to the site of the former aerodrome. At Shellness in 1909, the Short brothers built the first aeroplane factory in the United Kingdom and JTC Moore-Brabazon, later Lord Brabazon, created two national flying records. In 1922 the first Royal Naval Air Station was established there. Zeus armed with thunderbolts sits proud of a frieze of aircraft and the names of the men who established Sheppey's claim to be known as the cradle of Britain's aero industry.

A startling image of a biplane flying low over All Saints. It might be a Short No. 2, built at Messrs Short Brothers Aeroplane Factory at Shellness. A stained glass window in the church commemorates the lives of two pioneer airmen, Charles Rolls and Cecil Grace, who died in 1910 in separate flying accidents.

Spectators are kept well away from a Nieuport monoplane waiting to enter the Gordon Bennett Aviation race in July 1911. Mechanics check the aircraft under watchful official eyes.

Between events, spectators wander among the hangars. By 1912 Shorts had moved their factory from Shellness to this more suitable terrain at Eastchurch.

Close inspection of the Baby Wright biplane is permitted, July 1911. The Gordon Bennett Race attracted thousands of spectators who came to the island by road and rail. The winding roads to Eastchurch must have been unusually crowded, while the profits of the Sheppey Light Railway Company soared.

The general appearance of the people watching a Nieuport flying past gives the impression of a VIP enclosure, July 1911.

Shurland Hall, Sheppey.

Shurland Hall, c. 1927. The facade of the handsome Tudor mansion that Sir Thomas Cheyne built between 1510 and 1518 mostly of materials brought from his dismantled castle at Chilham. King Henry VIII and Anne Boleyn visited Cheyne at Shurland in 1532. In recent years the hall has become more of a ruin than the picture reveals and is now supported by scaffolding. With co-operation between the hall's owner and English Heritage and Swale Borough Council, it is hoped that essential work will begin shortly on strengthening the structure and restoring part of the hall.

Shurland Hall was the last major building erected on a site which has carried a variety of structures since at least the ninth-century Danish invasion.

The crossroads in the centre of Eastchurch clearly signposted in the 1920s. The aviation memorial now dominates the corner where the white house on the left once stood. The road directly opposite the church which led to the aerodrome is now the route to HM Prison, Standford Hill.

The Crooked Billet, a public house on the corner of Warden Road c. 1906, was recently renamed The Shurland, a freehouse where Rigden's Fine Ales and Stout are no longer served.

Several buildings survive from the High Street scene of c1912; some with different shop names others with a change of function. A member of the Ellum family took the photograph of the low-flying aircraft on page 104. The sign of The Castle public house stands out clearly on the left.

In the distance on the right the sign of The Castle and on the left the churchyard, c. 1910. The buildings in the foreground have gone and Geo Corle, family grocer, has given way to a petrol station.

Looking from Eastchurch across the fields and marshes to the distant River Swale c. 1916.

Travelling on the Warden Road there seems to have been little change over the years since this card was written in 1950. The Wheatsheaf Inn, set back a few yards from the roadway invites the thirsty passer-by to halt for refreshment before exploring the east end of the island.

Nine
Warden

Warden Cliff, c. 1912, a wooden fence prevents people from going too near the edge. The ladies' fine clothes hardly seem suitable in such an exposed spot.

Warden Point.

The most serious effects of erosion on the north coast of Sheppey were at Warden Point where a hoard of Roman coins found 100 yards from the shore-line suggests that it has gone on for many generations. In the 1870s the parish church of St James was a ruin. In 1883 the foundations and the churchyard succumbed and gradually most of the old village of Warden disappeared. Separate landslides demolished outlying cottages and farms. Postcards produced in successive years chart the devastation as the cliff edge crept closer to the trees and eventually they were no longer photographed. It is a sobering experience to look down on the result of centuries of destruction.

THE LANE, WARDEN, ISLE OF SHEPPEY. 3276

This young boy standing outside his home c. 1916 could not have imagined that so much of his childhood surroundings would disappear in his lifetime.

BRIDGESTONE HOUSE, WARDEN POINT, ISLE OF SHEPPEY

Bridgestone House, once the Warden Point post office, with its telephone kiosk and pillar box on the left. The house must have been given its name in 1836 when one of the stones Delamark Banks brought from the old London Bridge to build a tower for the church of St James became part of the garden wall. The house still stands, derelict, perilously close to the crumbling cliff edge.

167. WARDEN MANOR

Warden Manor in the 1950s, when it was a Toc H holiday centre with its own facilities for religious services. Christian associations with the building continue through the presence there of the Monastery of the Sorrowful and Immaculate Heart of Mary. The manor dates from the sixteenth century although earlier references are known. Over the centuries structural alterations have changed both its interior and exterior appearance.

113

According to the writer of this card the dining room at Warden Manor c. 1952 was formerly the old stables. Horse brasses at the extreme right of the photograph decorate the fireplace, above it the nameplate from the locomotive *Mercury*. Paraffin-oil heaters supplement the open fire. A gingham cloth on the dining-table surrounded by handsome windsor chairs evoke memories of pleasant evenings round the piano after days spent in the fresh air.

Friends visiting Vic Martin, the Toc H superintendent at Warden Manor, were entertained by his absorbing passion for model railways. His sophisticated network of tracks and rolling-stock was worthy of British Rail's attention.

Ten
Leysdown

Coastguard houses at Leysdown. The X marks the camp of the 1st Marylebone Boy Scout Troop in June 1920.

LEYSDOWN CHURCH.

St Clement church in Leysdown was built in 1874 to designs by R Wheeler and pulled down in 1989. Although there is now no evidence of there ever having been a church building on this ancient site, the overgrown graveyard, which is gradually being cleared by men from one of the island's prisons, is approached through a modern memorial lych-gate.

In 1927 the enterprising William Collingridge served refreshments in Station Road with his family at hand to help. The dirt road was used by day-trippers who could rest here in the gardens, buy cigarettes and tobacco and, for their children, buckets and spades to play with on the sands. The more adventurous might book a Leysdown motor tour of Sheppey.

A tranquil scene c. 1930 when there were few cars and many trees.

The Promenade, Leysdown.   115006.

Early in this century the Sheppey Light Railway and then the motor car made Leysdown accessible to many more visitors from the mainland. The beach was close to the village and bathing in the sea clean and safe.

LEYSDOWN BEACH,

The umbrella was less likely to be protection from the sun than from the wind in what has always been a breezy spot. Smart changing huts, deck-chairs, as well as bathing costumes and towels for those who came unprepared for a swim, could be hired at the Beach Attendant's Office.

115036 The Bungaletts. Leysdown.

"Bungaletts" is the name given to this basic holiday accommodation, the 1920s equivalent of the mobile home. As there was no mains supply, drinking and washing water had to be brought in by cart, and the camp-site manager also organised sewage disposal.

LEYSDOWN   98629

Many families were content to pitch their tents at the Leysdown end of Warden Bay in the 1920s. An early morning dip made showers and wash-basins unnecessary. Rain was the signal to strike camp and go home.

Of all Sheppey's varied landscape perhaps the Leysdown area has undergone the greatest change. The family shops and small bungalows that lined Station Road have been altered beyond recognition. The road to the sea is now an avenue of entertainment palaces and fast-food cafes that cater for the denizens of the acres of caravans in the fields surrounding the village. To many the change is not a happy one, but the clear, fresh air and open countryside only minutes away make Leysdown a demi-paradise for people coming from overcrowded city streets and soulless suburbs.

One victim of the changes to the village was CJ Payne's Stores, a newsagent and general shop in Station Road c. 1938.

Advertised as "Kent's Best" c. 1930, the Rose and Crown in the centre of Leysdown is still a popular meeting-place.

From 1901 until 1950 the Sheppey Light Railway steamed across the island from Queenborough to the end of the line at Leysdown.

Multi-pictorial cards have always been popular for portraying the varied attractions of a particular place and its environs. This group is from the 1950s.

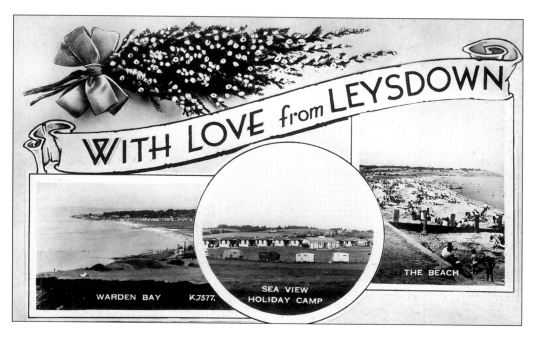

A LAZY CARD from LEYSDOWN-ON-SEA

Weather Nice	✓		Raining Again	
Food Good	✓		Home Cooking's Best	
Accommodation Good	✓		Let Me Out of Jail !	
Fit as a Fiddle	✓		All Aches and Pains	
Wish You Were Here	✓		Managing Without You	
Been Swimming			Hate Neat Water	
Drinking Steadily		✓	On the Waggon	
Send Some Money		✓	Don't Need Money	
Coming Here Again	✓		Only by Force	
Caught a Girl			Caught a Fish	
Caught a Boy			Caught a Cold	
Met Nice People	✓		Met Some Shockers	
Liking The Place	✓		Hate Every Minute	
Do All My Work			Leave All My Work	
Been Sightseeing	✓		Not Budged an Inch	
Air is Invigorating	✓		Sleeping All Day	
Seeing Life Here	✓		Bored to Tears	
Will Write Again		✓	You'll Hear Nothing More	

TICK WHERE APPLICABLE

The "lazy card" purports to save the sender the trouble of writing at length about a holiday's pros and cons. This writer and his family seem more than satisfied with their holiday at Leysdown-on-Sea in September 1964.

The road east from Leysdown leads eventually to Shell Ness. On the way it passes the site of the Short brothers' first aeroplane factory. After a visit, two other famous flying brothers, William and Orville Wright spoke of "the very nice flying ground at Sheppey Island".

Eleven
Harty and Elmley

The church of St Thomas the Apostle at Harty, which dates from the eleventh century, is often referred to as the remotest church in Kent. Without electricity, its faithful congregation still worship by the light of candles and oil-lamps.

Edward Hasted's map of 1795 shows the Isle of Harty and the Isle of Emly as sparsely-inhabited parishes, with ditches criss-crossing miles of desolate marshland. Each had its own ferry service to mainland Kent but was separated by dykes and creeks one from the other and from the rest of Sheppey. Today Harty and Elmley are integral parts of the island and, while neither ferry now runs, the Ferry Inn at Harty still welcomes travellers. A few farms remain, some ruins and, as becomes the island's name, many sheep. This southern

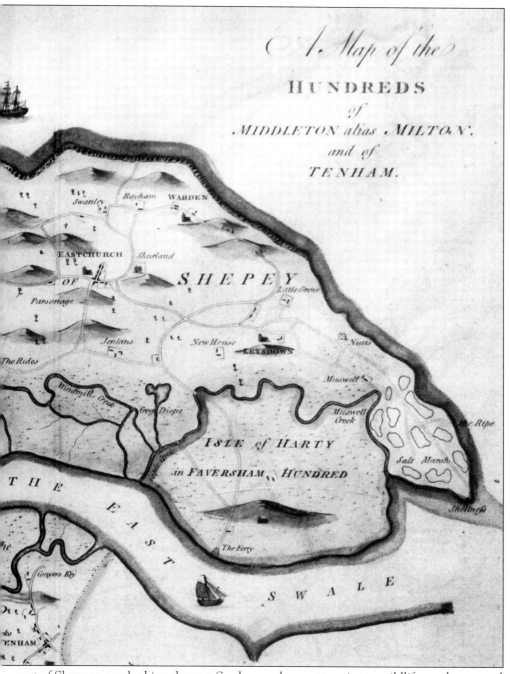

A Map of the

HUNDREDS

of

MIDDLETON alias MILTON.

and of

TENHAM.

part of Sheppey overlooking the east Swale was always attractive to wildlife as a haven and a larder. A varied habitat set in such isolation makes it an ideal home for a huge variety of fauna and flora, particularly birds: over 200 species have been recorded at the Elmley Marshes reserve. Investment by the Royal Society for the Protection of Birds secures these 3,000 ecologically rich and fascinating ~~areas~~ acres from possible depredation by the out-of-town supermarket, the theme-park or - more seriously - yet another caravan-site.

For two thousand years Sheppey, this "isle of sheep", has borne the same name, albeit in different tongues. To the Romans it was *Insula Ovium*, *Scéapige* to the invading Saxons, *Het Eylandt Shepey* to de Ruyter's raiders.